Checkmate made EASY

Wrriten by — Dr. Hoot

Published in 2024 by Skooler Books

Checkmate made Easy

Skooler Books

ISBN: 9789334271447

Dedicated to

ALL

GOOD BOYS

Hi Kids

Ready to unlock the secrets of the most epic game ever?

Dive into a world where animated chess pieces come alive to teach you their moves and strategies!
Let's learn, laugh and master chess together.

How to Play

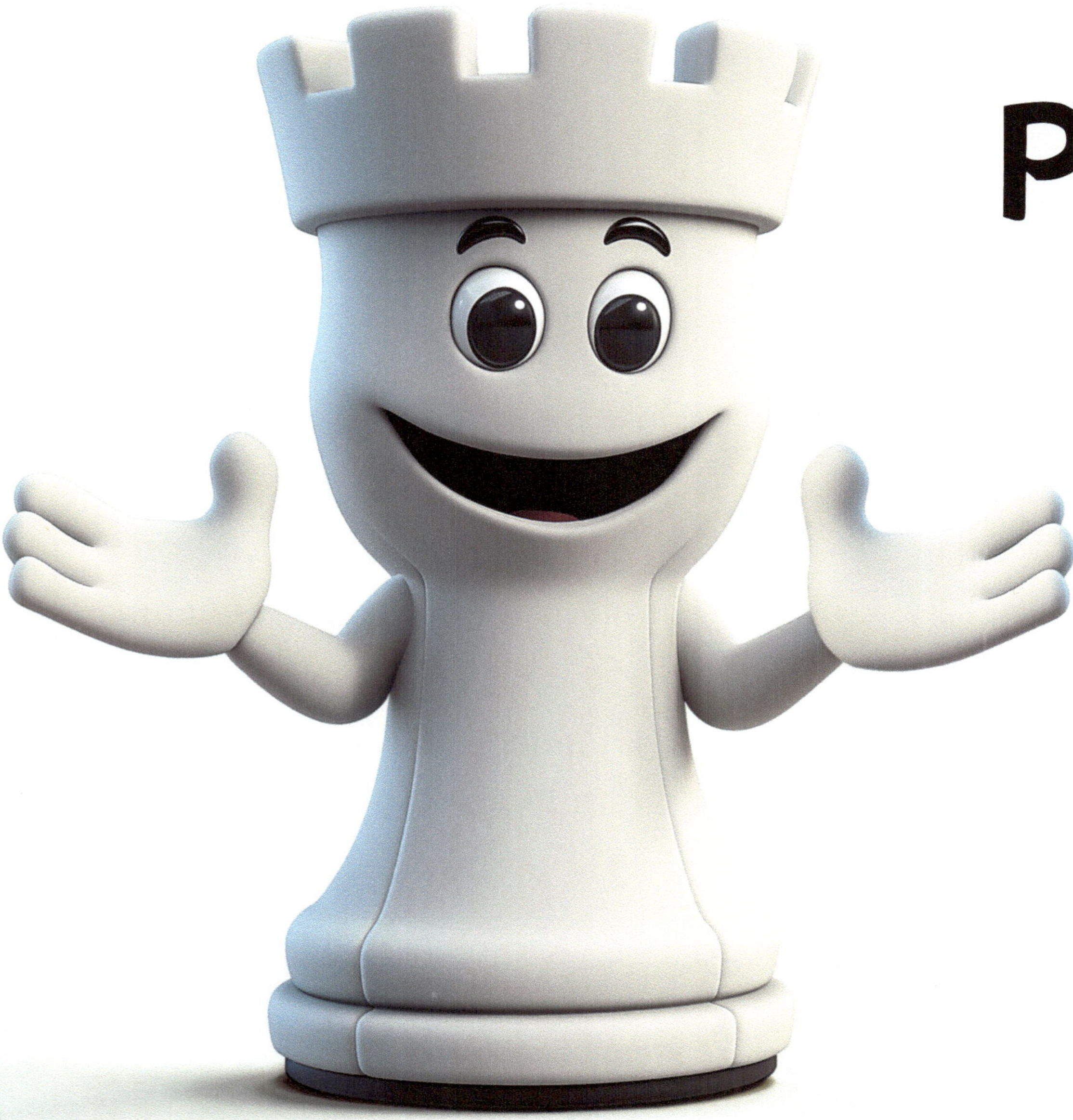

In chess, there are two teams: one side plays with white pieces, and the other with black. Each player starts with an army of 16 pieces.Your mission is to outsmart your opponent and protect your king while trying to capture theirs!

Now, look below and check out how the pieces are set up before the game begins.

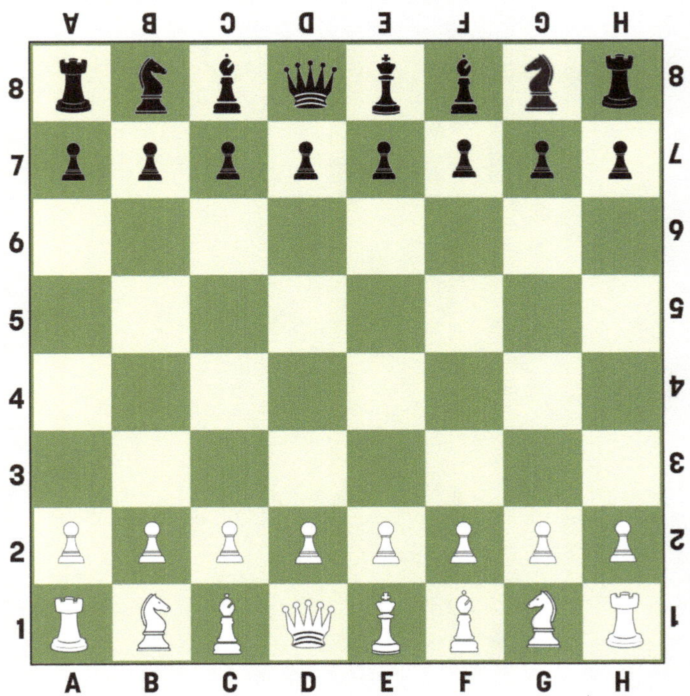

Chester -the- Pawn

Meet Chester the pawn, always ready to take his first step into battle. Chester has a special gift- on his very first move, he can step forward one square or take a leap of two! After that, it's one step at a time.

When it's time to capture, he moves diagonally, sneaking past opponents with a sidestep.

Move

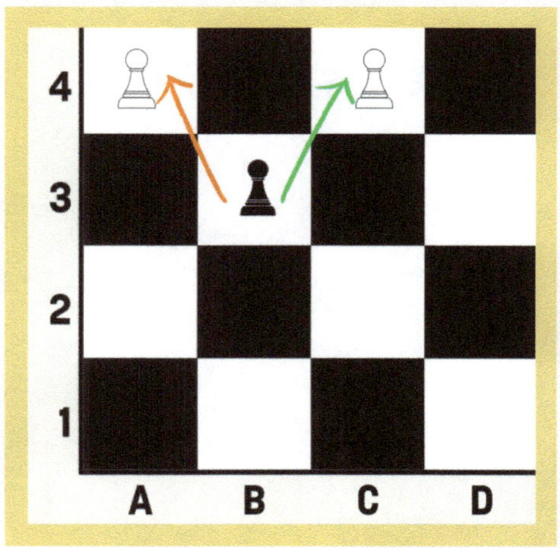

Attack

Harry
-the-
Knight

Meet Harry the Knight, the trickiest mover on the chessboard! Harry doesn't go straight like the others; he hops in an 'L' shape: two steps in one direction and one step to the side. He loves to leap over pieces, making him the board's ultimate jumper!

L Shape

Ricky -the- Rook

Meet Ricky the Rook–he's the straight shooter of the chessboard! Ricky loves long walks, but only in straight lines. He zooms up, down, and side to side, as far as the board allows, but never diagonally. Keep his path clear, and Ricky's ready to rule the board!

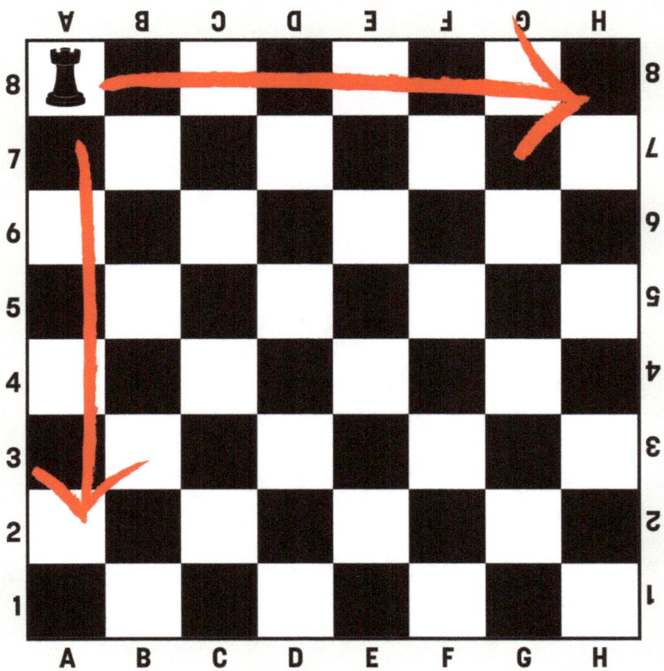

Glider
-the-
Bishop

Meet Bishop the Glider, the swift strategist of the chessboard! He moves diagonally across the board, sliding gracefully through open spaces. With his sharp angles and long reach, the Bishop is always ready to outmaneuver and surprise his opponents!

Leo -the- King

Meet King Leo, the ruler of the chessboard! King Leo moves carefully, stepping just one square at a time in any direction: up, down, sideways, or diagonally. He may be slow, but every move counts–protect him at all costs!

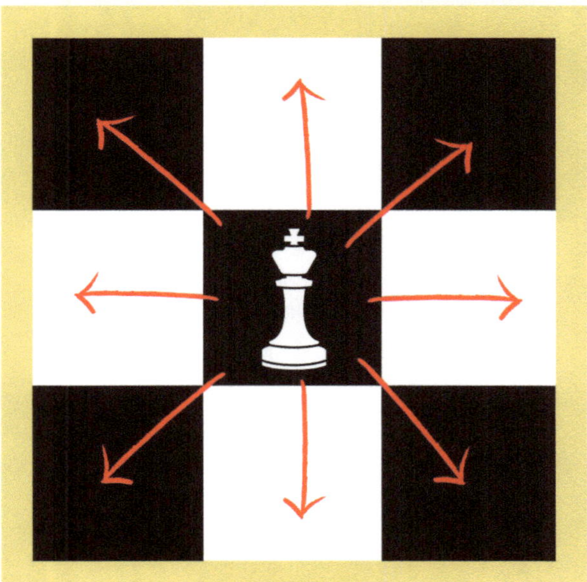

Bella
-the-
Queen

Meet Bella the Queen, the most powerful piece on the chessboard! She moves with grace and authority, gliding in any direction–straight, sideways, or diagonal–as far as her path is clear. With Bella on your side, victory is always within reach!

En - Passant

Let me tell you about a sneaky little chess trick called en passant–it's French for 'in passing'! Imagine this: your pawn is marching forward, and the opponent's pawn tries to zoom past yours by moving two squares on its first turn. If that happens, your pawn can say, 'Not so fast!' and capture it, just like it had only moved one square. But here's the catch: you have to make the capture right away, or the chance is gone forever. It's like a secret move only pawns know!

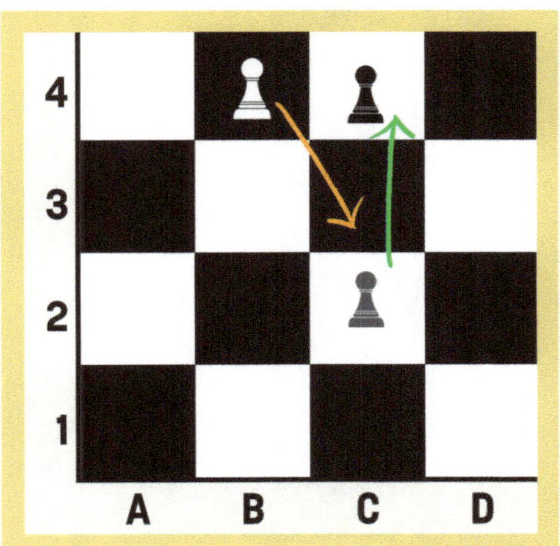

Castling

Castling is a super cool move where the king and a rook work together! The king takes a tiny step, moving two squares toward the rook, and the rook hops over the king. But remember, there can't be any pieces in the way, and the king needs to stay in the same spot until then!

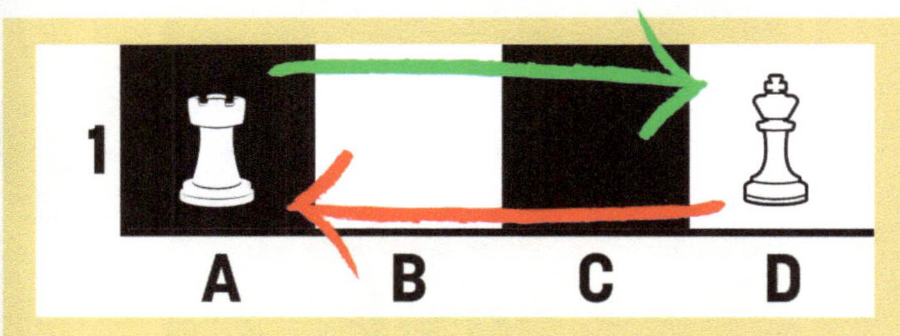

Kingside

Queenside

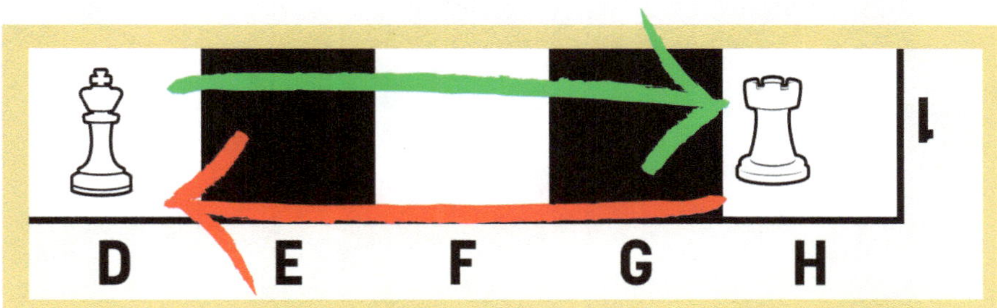

Promotion

Hey, did you hear about the little pawn with big dreams? Guess what, it has a superpower! If it bravely marches to the other end of the board, it can transform into something amazing. A mighty queen, a sneaky knight, or even a tower of strength. What would you become if you had that power? Ready to cheer the pawn on?

Crack the Chess Code

- **The Board Letters and Numbers**: The chessboard has columns labeled a to h (left to right) and rows numbered 1 to 8 (bottom to top). Each square has a name, like e4 or b7.

- **Piece Names**: Each piece is represented by a letter:

King = K
Queen = Q
Rook = R
Bishop = B
Knight = N

- **How Moves Are Written**:

  Piece + Destination Square: For example, if a knight moves to f3, it's written as Nf3.

  For pawns, just write the square, like e4.

- **Captures**: If a piece captures, add an "x". For example:

  A knight capturing on f3 is Nxf3.

  A pawn capturing on d5 is exd5 (the "e" tells where the pawn came from).

- **Special Moves**:

  Castling: King-side castling is 0-0, and Queen-side castling is 0-0-0.

  Promotion: When a pawn reaches the last rank, write the move plus the piece it becomes, like e8=Q (pawn promotes to queen).

  Check: Add a "+" for check, like Qh5+.

  Checkmate: Add a "#" for checkmate, like Qg7#.

Please leave a

Review

www.ingramcontent.com/pod-product-compliance
Lightning Source LLC
Chambersburg PA
CBHW061316170726
48282CB00020B/116
9789334271447